Hungry
Craving Jesus in Recovery From an Eating Disorder

Staci Luker

Copyright © 2016 Staci Luker

All rights reserved.

ISBN- 10: 152394191X
ISBN-13: 978-1523941919

DEDICATION

This book is dedicated to anyone who feels stuck in that dark abyss. I hope that reading this book will encourage you as you discover that when you feel that you don't have the strength to stand, there is One waiting to hold you up.

CONTENTS

	Acknowledgments	I
1	Finding Fellowship	14
2	The Jesus of Miracles	21
3	The Lies We Believe	34
4	Surrender isn't Easy	49
5	Girl Lost	65
6	Picking Grapes	73
7	Fear	81
8	Breaking Down Walls	88
9	Only Jesus	95
10	The Voices We Hear	102
11	Breaking Plates	109
12	Get Ready for Battle	116

ACKNOWLEDGMENTS

Jesus. Without Him, I am nothing and I can do nothing apart from Him. Thank you to my family and friends who stood beside me through the rollercoaster of my eating disorder and recovery. A Center for Eating Disorders in Birmingham, AL: Your treatment method is amazing and I can never thank you all for the amazing work that you do. To my family at Shades Mountain Baptist Church, thank you for welcoming me when I was so broken and being supportive as God mended my brokenness and for rejoicing with me over His victories in my life.

PROCEED WITH CAUTION

For those that want to know, I wanted to provide a backstory on how my eating disorder began and what triggered it. The goal here is not sympathy, and really not even understanding specifics of my own story. The goal in my sharing this section of the book is to propel an understanding among readers who have not experienced an eating disorder that it's not about the food.

No one wakes up one morning and decides they want an eating disorder. It is a miserable disease that affects you mentally, emotionally, and physically. It is the number one killer among mental health disorders and it affects so many people, both men and women, young and old.

This section will mention sexual assault, so please, if that is triggering to you, skip to chapter one. You won't be lost by skipping this section. In fact, tear these pages out if you want.

My life was a perfect storm for an eating disorder to develop. I was a perfectionist, demanding perfection from myself. If my best wasn't an A or a 4.0, it wasn't acceptable. Many people with eating disorders are perfectionists in some way. Mine was projected on my school work. I found my identity in being "the smart girl".

In June of 2007, a few months shy of my seventeenth birthday and already well into those awkward teenage years of trying to figure out who you are and trying to fit in all at the same time, I experienced sexual violence at the hands of a complete stranger whose face was stuck in the forefront of my mind for way too long. Because of the victim blaming culture that we live in, I assumed that it was my fault and it must have been something I had done or was wearing. I thought that if I told anyone, then I would be the one who was punished. While driving home, I made the decision that I would not be forced to tell this story over and over again.

So I drove home, got in the shower, and tried unsuccessfully to sleep until it was time for me to wake up and get ready for my summer babysitting job. Life would go on, no one would know what happened, and I would pretend like nothing had happened.

The only problem was, that didn't work, and it never would have worked. In order for me to carry this out, it meant that every thing I was feeling got stuffed down inside so that it wasn't visible to anyone around me. The problem with that is that those feelings don't disappear. They simply built up until I had nowhere else to stuff them.

It didn't take long for me to become so full of these packed up feelings that it started to affect me physically and I didn't want to eat. The only thing I wanted to do was lie in the bed and wish it would end. I didn't want to sleep because I was tormented by nightmares. During the day, it replayed in my mind and I never knew what little thing would trigger a replay so real that it felt like it was happening all over again.

Soon people began to notice that I wasn't

eating and started to say something to me. Though they were coming from a place of concern, to me it felt like a threat. Someone had taken control of my body from me already and it turned my world upside down. No one else was going to control my body by telling me what I had to eat.

That was when food became a way for me to regain a sense of control in my life. That was the point that my eating disorder turned from a dull roar to an overwhelming turmoil in my life. I may have lost control of my body that night, but no more. I would now control what went in and out of my body by restricting food, over exercising, and for a brief time, purging. In order to survive day-to-day life, I needed to feel like I had control over my body.

It worked; at least for a little while. Then, the area in which I had turned in order to gain control, quickly stole that control. Once again, I found myself with no control over my body. The only difference was that my body was now controlled my anorexia and the fight to get it back would be a decade long uphill battle in which the victory flag was only claimed when the position of Commander-in-Chief was shifted from myself to Jesus.

Hungry

CHAPTER 1
FINDING FELLOWSHIP

A few days before I checked into what I knew would be my final eating disorder treatment facility, I found myself with a few hours to pass after I had checked out of my hotel room and while I waited to pick up some paperwork. I really did not have a desire to do anything, so I found myself driving aimlessly around Birmingham. As I was driving, I came across a church that caught my attention with its large, round, beautiful window looking out over the passersby. As I slowed down to take a look, I could feel God telling me to stop.

"Here?" I asked.

"Yes. Just park and walk in."

"Oh God, I can't do that. It's the middle of the week and I don't know anyone here. They'll see my struggles all over my face."

"Just trust Me."

So I pulled into the parking lot and put my car in park. I would love to tell you that I stepped out of my car and walked inside that church with prompt, straightforward obedience, but that was not the case. Instead, I continued to push back against God.

"Okay. I'm here. But there is no way that I am getting out of my car."

"Do you trust Me?"

"Yes, but look at me! I'm such a mess. I don't even know how I ended up here in Birmingham with just my car and my suitcase in the trunk. Lord, I am not worthy of walking in that door. I need to protect people from seeing this dark abyss that I live in."

Silence.

"Do you trust Me?"

"Lord, I told You that I do..."

And then I remembered that three letter word that I had inserted after my answer: "but". That small word that is so often overlooked as a necessary conjunction, but definitely not that significant, had told an entirely different story. In that three letter conjunction, I had said so much. God took that one word and showed me that what I was really saying was, "I know I should trust You. I want to trust You. But I am afraid to surrender my control. I'm afraid to trust".

I would like to say that trust is a one-time decision that carries over indefinitely, but it's not. We trust in Jesus as our personal Savior, but if we aren't trusting Him with every aspect of our lives, moment by moment, then we are missing out on the abundant life that He has in store for us.

From that moment in that day, I surrendered that control and (slowly) made my way to the office doors of Shades Mountain Baptist Church and it was right where I needed to be.

Jesus brought me directly to godly people who were willing to meet me where I was as I began the long climb out of the deep, dark abyss that I had been hiding in for so long.

"You don't have to stay down there all alone. Take My hand."

The Lord is a stronghold for the oppressed, a stronghold in times of trouble. And those who know Your name put their trust in You, for You, O Lord, have not forsaken those who seek You.
Psalm 9:9-10

Blessed is the man who trusts in the Lord, whose trust is in the Lord. He is like a tree planted by water, that sends out its roots by the stream, and does not fear when heat comes, for its leaves remain green, and is not anxious in the year of drought, for it does not cease to bear fruit.
Jeremiah 17:7-8

If you are reading this, maybe you are still hiding out in that abyss of pain that has become your comfort zone. Maybe you have started the climb out, but you are growing weary and struggling to see the freedom that glimmers over the ledge. Maybe you have already reached the ledge of recovery or you have a loved one that is still trapped in the crashing waves of an eating disorder.

Cling to these words of truth: He knows.

He knows every ounce of pain. He knows and sees every tear. He knows that you feel overcome by shame and doubt and fear, and that sometimes you just feel worthless. He knows.

And His heart breaks for you because He also knows your worth.

He sees you as a treasure to be cherished and He knows the joy that comes when you believe that about yourself as a child of God.

For You formed my inward parts; You knitted me together in my mother's womb. I praise You, for I am fearfully and wonderfully made. Wonderful are Your works; my soul knows it very well. My frame was not hidden from You , when I was being made in secret, intricately woven in the

depths of the earth. Your eyes saw my unformed substance; in Your book were written, every one of them, the days that were formed for me, when as yet there were none of them.
   Psalm 139:13-16

He knows what is in your life that is holding you back from believing that. He knows the trauma, and the hurt, and the loss. He knows every moment that has forever altered your life. He knows.

Not only does He know, He *understands*.

He knows you intimately, inside and out, far better than you even know yourself.

He waits with open arms, longing to wrap them around you. He longs to bring healing to those wounds that you carry and to see you experience what it means to find beauty in the broken. He longs to see you joyously living out the abundant life that He has had planned for you all along.

"For I know the plans I have for you," says the Lord, "plans to prosper you, and not to harm you,

to give you a hope and a future."
   Jeremiah 29:11

He longs for you to believe what He already knows about you. He wants you to look the enemy in the eye and say "NO. MORE."

No longer will you steal my life from me.

No longer will you be given any power here.

No longer will you be allowed to shame and devalue me.

No longer will you be allowed to make me feel like anything less than the loved, beautiful, cherished, and treasured child of the King that I am.

No more.

It's time to take your life back. It's time to claim your identity in Christ as His beloved, adopted child.

It's time to be set free.

CHAPTER 2
THE JESUS OF MIRACLES

I feel a tug on the bottom of my dress as we stand in line at a local ice cream shop waiting to place our orders. My eyes venture down to see my curly red headed toddler pointing to all of the ice cream flavors, excitedly (and very loudly) proclaiming, "Look, Momma! Look!"

With as much animation as I could muster, I mirrored her enthusiasm as we made our way past rows and rows of flavors to choose from. She settled on one as I continued to narrow down the flavors I would choose from.

This was a new adventure. Months before, I would be postponing the inevitable and doing anything I could to avoid having to order ice cream as I was consumed by the thoughts of the calories the ice cream held and my warped belief of what those calories would do to my malnourished body. I would be telling myself that I didn't deserve that ice cream because I was damaged and broken. Ice cream was a treat.

This visit was different. I was instead, trying to rush myself along, as I went back and forth over which flavor I would choose because they all sounded amazing. This time, as I made my way down the rows and rows of ice cream, I didn't hate my body or myself. Sharing ice cream with my family is a fun treat, and not a scary, dreaded outing.

Sure, those thoughts try to creep up. But they have no power or place in my life. Not anymore. Not today.

Months before this moment, I never thought I would be here. It didn't seem possible that I would ever be able to go out with my family for ice cream, or any meal, and enjoy it. But mostly, I didn't believe that I could ever love my body, love myself, or accept the love of others.

Yet here I am. I'm here because I serve a God who can; a God of miracles.

Jesus loves you.

We hear this truth a lot. It is a truth that we speak often. As children we sing the familiar children's song, "Jesus loves me", and we read about His love within His Word. It is a truth whose importance is beyond any words that I could pen on this paper, or speak with my lips, or even begin to think of in my mind.

How often do we say, "Jesus loves you" out of habit rather than out of heartfelt conviction? How many times do we hear this and say we believe it when in reality we hold our steel armor so steady and strong against this truth instead of letting it penetrate the armor and break it down?

How often do we speak those words yet never let them permeate our soul?

We all do it. Every day. I read and hear and speak this truth at least once a day in which I do not actually sit and let the magnitude of it sink in and grow roots.

If you are reading this, I want you to know, to *truly* know, that Jesus loves you.

Take two minutes right now and reflect on that truth in your own heart before you read any further.

How does it make you feel to know that the God of all the universe truly and sincerely loves you?

On that day, when evening had come, He said to them, "Let us go across to the other side." And leaving the crowd, they took Him with them in the boat, just as He was. And other boats were with Him. And a great windstorm arose, and the waves were breaking into the boat, so that the boat was already filling. But He was in the stern, asleep on the cushion. And they woke Him and said to Him, "Teacher, do you not care that we are perishing?" And He awoke and rebuked the wind and said to the sea, "Peace! Be still!" And the wind ceased, and there was a great calm. He said to them, "Why are you so afraid? Have you

still no faith?" And they were filled with great fear and said to one another, "Who then is this, that even the wind and the sea obey Him?"
Mark 4:35-41 (ESV)

This Jesus who calms the sea, who speaks and the wind and sea obey Him, loves you. He loves you more than every drop in that sea. He loves you more than the power within that wind.

And there was a woman who had had a discharge of blood for twelve years, and who had suffered much under many physicians, and had spent all that she had, and was no better but rather grew worse. She had heard the reports about Jesus and came up behind Him in the crowd and touched His garment. For she said, "If I touch even His garments, I will be made well." And immediately the flow of blood dried up, and she felt in her body that she was healed of her disease. And Jesus, perceiving in Himself that power had gone out from Him, immediately turned about in the crowd and said, "Who touched my garments?" And His disciples said to Him, "You see the crowd pressing around You, and yet You say, 'Who touched me?'" And He looked around to see who had done it. But the

woman, knowing what had happened to her, came in fear and trembling and fell down before Him and told Him the whole truth. And He said to her, "Daughter, your faith has made you well; go in peace, and be healed of your disease."
Mark 5:25-34 (ESV)

This Jesus who healed a woman who had been suffering for years when she sought just to touch His cloak, loves you.

And as Jesus passed on from there, two blind men followed Him, crying aloud, "Have mercy on us, Son of David." When He entered the house, the blind men came to Him, and Jesus said to them, "Do you believe that I am able to do this?" They said to Him, "Yes, Lord." Then He touched their eyes, saying, "According to your faith be it done to you." And their eyes were opened. And Jesus sternly warned them, "See that no one knows about it." But they went away and spread His fame through all that district.
Matthew 9: 27-31 (ESV)

This Jesus who caused the blind to see, loves you. His love for you is beyond the beauty and magnitude of everything He created on earth for us to see and enjoy. It doesn't even touch His love for you.

Lifting up His eyes, then, and seeing that a large crowd was coming toward Him, Jesus said to Philip, "Where are we to buy bread so that these people may eat?" He said this to test him, for He Himself knew what He would do. Philip answered Him, "Two hundred denarii would not buy enough bread for each of them to get a little." One of His disciples, Andrew, Simon Peter's brother, said to Him, "There is a boy here who has five barley loaves and two fish, but what are they for so many?" Jesus said, "Have the people sit down." Now there was much grass in the place. So the men sat down, about five thousand in number. Jesus then took the loaves, and when He had given thanks, He distributed them to those who were seated. So also the fish, as much as they wanted. And when they had eaten their fill, He told His disciples, "Gather up the leftover fragments that nothing may be lost." So they gathered them up and filled twelve baskets with fragments from their five barley loaves left by those who had eaten. When the people saw the sign that He had done, they said, "This is indeed the Prophet who is to come into the world!"

John 6: 5-14 (ESV)

This Jesus who fed five thousand with five loaves and two fish loves you. This Jesus who magnifies, will equip you and provide for you because He loves you.

Immediately He made the disciples get into the boat and go before Him to the other side, while He dismissed the crowds. And after He dismissed the crowds, He went up onto the mountain by Himself to pray. When evening came, He was there alone, but the boat by this time was a long way from the land, beaten by the waves, for the wind was against them. And in the fourth watch of the night, He came to them, walking on the sea. But when the disciples saw Him walking on the sea, they were terrified, and said, "It is a ghost!" and they cried out in fear. But immediately Jesus spoke to them saying, "Take Heart; it is I. Do not be afraid."

And Peter answered Him, "Lord if it is You, command me to come to you on the water." He said, "Come." So Peter got out of the boat and walked on the water and came to Jesus. But when he saw the wind he was afraid, and beginning to sink he cried out, "Lord, save me." Jesus

immediately reached out His hand and took hold of him, saying to him, "O you of little faith, why did you doubt?" And when they got into the boat, the wind ceased. And those in the boat worshiped Him, saying, "Truly You are the Son of God."
    Matthew 14:22-33 (ESV)

This Jesus who walked on water, loves you. This Jesus who defied physics, who still reached out His hand in rescue when doubt crept up, loves you. His hand will always reach out to you. Always.

Then He returned from the region of Tyre and went through Sidon to the Sea of Galilee, in the region of the Decapolis. And they brought to Him a man who was deaf and had a speech impediment, and they begged Him to lay His hand on him. And taking him aside from the crowd privately, He put His fingers into his ears and after spitting touched his tongue. And looking up to heaven, He sighed and said to him "Ephphatha," that is, "Be opened." And his ears were opened, his tongue was released, and he spoke plainly. And Jesus charged them to tell no one. But the more He charged them, the more zealously they proclaimed it. And they were

astonished beyond measure, saying, "He has done all things well. He even makes the deaf hear and the mute speak."
    Mark 7:31-37 (ESV)

This Jesus who caused the deaf to hear, loves you.

He walked to Calvary with you in mind. Don't just read that and then close this book without letting that sink in and penetrate every part of your heart. Let that grow roots deep within your soul that cannot be shaken. Hold on to that truth and it will withstand any storm and anything that life sends your way.

The God of the universe, the Jesus you just read about; He loves you. He doesn't just love you a little. He loves you well beyond our capacity to love or even to understand. He desires to spend time with you. He wants you to let Him into every part of your life.

This Jesus who we will one day witness all of heaven and earth bow down to in praise chooses to call you His beloved child.

One of the greatest obstacles that stands between an eating disorder and recovery is pride. Pride says that you can reach recovery on your own. Pride says that you can end your eating disorder any time that you choose, even though you have probably already tried and failed at that. Pride tells you that you are invincible and that your eating disorder won't hurt you. Pride will tell you that you are fine and that you don't need help or recovery.

Pride lies. Pride blocks the view of what God sees in you because pride hides self-hatred and allows it to exist.

Recovery requires you to learn to love yourself, flaws and all, which is such a foreign concept to most people who struggle with an eating disorder. Recovery requires you to bring that self-hatred to the light and examine it. Recovery requires you to dig down deep to understand how it got there so that you can cut it off at the roots.

True humility is the bridge between that self-hatred hiding pride and recovery.

I am not talking about a skewed definition of humility that tells you that you have to beat yourself down in order to build others up. True humility requires loving yourself. True humility provides a clear view of how God sees you as His beloved child. True humility sees and accepts your own worth and value as a unique, handcrafted, child of God and knows that every single person possesses that same worth and value, whether they sleep in a palace or in a prison cell. True humility says that you can sit at the table with everyone else because you are not less than them, but equal. While humility sometimes entails thinking of yourself less, it never means thinking less of yourself.

Humility is not putting yourself on a lower level than everyone else when doing so requires you to go against everything that God says about you and your worth. Put everyone on the same level. Everyone sits together. You're not above, but at the same time, you are never below. It's a level ground and everyone sits level with each other.

If you ever feel like recovery is not possible for you, call that lie out right then, on the spot.

On your own, it probably isn't, but with Jesus all things are possible. This Jesus you just read about, who loves you more than we can comprehend, can do anything.

But Jesus looked at them and said, "With man this is impossible, but with God all things are possible."
Matthew 19:26 (ESV)

CHAPTER 3
THE LIES WE BELIEVE

A dark, ominous cloud lingers at the end of the dim hallway that I have found myself in. It is frightening and I want to turn around and bolt in the opposite direction. No matter how hard I try, my legs continue to move towards the cloud, one step at a time, and I have no control over my legs. They continue to take one step after another despite all of my efforts to cease their progress.

That loss of control is my greatest fear. Without control, I'm walking towards a cloud that contains all of the trauma from my past and the possibility of being hurt in the same ways again.

Suddenly, my legs stop and I'm no longer moving towards the cloud. Instead, I am frozen in place as I hear music begin to play in the distance. The music grows louder and I begin to decipher the words, recognizing the familiar tune of Amazing Grace that I had sung along to so many times in church. I'm confused as I turn my head all around trying to determine where it's coming from, as my legs remain frozen in place. The volume of the music continues to increase and the lyrics continue to pour forth, gradually growing louder with each passing verse.

Finally, I slowly open my eyes and see the light of the rising sun beginning to peek through the blinds of the window beside my bed. The music from the alarm clock on my phone continues to play and grow louder by the second. I slide my finger across the screen of my phone to turn the alarm off and I lie there looking out my window at the trees surrounding the top of the building where I am currently spending the majority of my days.

I groan as I roll over and start to untangle myself from all of the blankets on my bed. I do not want to get out of the bed. I do not want to face the day or deal with my life. Reluctantly I step out of bed, leaving behind a tangle of sheets and blankets that I don't have the energy to straighten, and throw on some leggings and a baggy t-shirt that reaches my knees. I want my body hidden from the world and myself. I am ashamed it of it. I hate it.

I brush my teeth and throw my hair in a messy bun on top of my head. Makeup is ignored because it seems pointless. There is nothing that could make me look any better. I grab my pink and white striped backpack and toss in my iPod and my journal along with a book to read.

My footsteps are slow and dragging because I know that a plate full of breakfast that I don't want to eat is waiting for me in the building next door. The warmth of the sun as I step out of the door is a sharp contrast to the air-conditioned house I am leaving. I pause in it for a second and take it in because I know I will be cold again once I step inside. I'm always cold. My body is too starved to warm itself.

With a frown on my face, I sit down at the dining table to do my morning paperwork and I wear my pain like a badge that I have earned the right to wear; it's exhausting, but it's comfortable because it's what I know.

People speak to me as they pass and I make just enough movement with my head to acknowledge that they spoke. I do not want to look up and speak or smile; I don't deserve that exchange with other people. I have destined myself to be forever trapped in the pain and sorrow of my past because it is my punishment for being tarnished.

A week ago I left my home and my husband and kids and drove myself to this eating disorder treatment center a few hours from the place I called home to try to finally get better and deal with the pain from my past. I hope it works, but I am incredibly skeptical.

The smell of scrambled eggs makes its way into the dining room amidst the sounds of clanking silverware and people shuffling around each other in the kitchen. I'm not allowed in the kitchen at all yet, which is frustrating because my need for control hates having to wait for people to do things for me, but at the same time, the thought of being in that kitchen is terrifying.

The seemingly endless mound of morning paperwork does eventually end and I get up from the table to place it in the manila folder by the door to the nurse's office. Regular Monday morning routine requires that I knock on the door to let them do my weekly weigh-in. I hear the deadbolt turn and the door opens for me to step in. I undress and slip on a gown, then open the bathroom door. The nurse places the scale on the floor in the bathroom and I step on it with no idea the number that the scale settles on because the numbers appear on a small screen on the other side of the wall out of my sight.

A little anger wells up inside of me because I desperately want to know what that number is. In one week, I feel like I have gained fifty pounds from all of the food that this place is making me eat. I have gone from weighing myself upwards of ten times a day to not seeing my weight at all for an entire week.

Breakfast is on the table when I step back through the door to the medication room. Other clients are seated while one passes out silverware and the dietician settles down with her own breakfast at the end of the table. Begrudgingly, I take a seat in front of my plate and stare at the scrambled eggs while I draw circles around them with my fork. Grapes, cashews, and almond milk surround them and I feel nauseous as I realize that I have to eat every bite or drink a chalky supplement that already make me cringe when I see them.

The battle in my mind is already raging and it's barely eight o'clock in the morning. I know that physically I need to eat because I haven't eaten since dinner last night, but I already feel so full and the plate in front of me contains what would have previously been at least a couple of days worth of food for me. After nine years of being very deep in a struggle with anorexia, I don't even remember what it feels like to be hungry.

I replace the fork in my hand with a blue pen to record my feelings of anger and fear before the meal. This is something we are required to do, but I am writing slowly and drawing it out to put off having to take a bite of the food. Reluctantly, the fork is back in my hand and I can feel the eyes of the dietician looking to see if I've eaten anything as I stare at the plate and fight the tears that are trying to make their way from my tired, droopy eyes.

The battle rages on.

You can't eat all of that food. You are already huge. Soon you won't even be able to wear your clothes anymore. That's way too much food for you.

I try to counteract the lies by reminding myself that this is a normal portion of food for someone with my body type and that my dietician knows what she is doing when she writes out my meal plans. Actually believing that, though, requires giving trust that I don't have to give right now.

How can you trust them? They just want to take your control away. You remember what has happened in the past when you didn't have control, don't you? You always end up hurt. You need to keep a tight grip on that control. There is no way you can eat this food.

I hear mention of a supplement from the end

of the table and I suddenly realize how much I do *not* want to drink that chalky drink. I have to choose between that and the food. I dig my fork into the scrambled eggs and begin shoveling the food in my mouth as fast as I can; not because I am hungry, but because I want to eat it fast enough that I don't have to taste the food and that I don't have to think about it as much while I eat it. If I let myself think about it in the moment, I will never be able to finish it and then I will still end up having to drink a supplement.

A clattering sound shatters the silence that filled my spot at the table as I drop my fork onto the blue ceramic plate that held the breakfast I just devoured in mere minutes. The food is inside of me and I don't have to fear drinking the supplement. Instead, I wish I could die. Physically, I feel like I will quite literally explode and I fear that the food is going to make its way back up my throat at any moment.

I sit on my hands and tap my legs up and down as fast as I can because I know that if I let myself stand up, I will bolt to the bathroom to make myself throw up. That's not usually a temptation for me anymore, but right now I am desperate to remove this food from my body and knowing that I can't do that ignites a fear inside of me that torments my mind.

I feel out of control, and I feel afraid.

Even as those around me stand and take the empty plates into the kitchen to wash them, I don't have the opportunity to bolt to the bathroom. I am still on "observation" and have to sit with a staff member until it's time for us to have our first group session for the day.

I feel my blood pulsing through my body as the anger inside of me builds. The more out of control I feel, the more afraid I become, and the fear is fueling the anger. The tears well up in my eyes and I am not sure which emotion they are a result of. I only know that to let them roll down my cheek is to be vulnerable and I clench my jaws together as I choke them back inside.

There is one thing that every single eating disorder has in common: they lie. Sometimes the lies are ones that we tell ourselves and sometimes they are lies that we tell those around us.

The lies that we tell others start out innocently enough. At least, that is what we tell ourselves. Eventually, you will lose control over them and lose track of them as the eating disorder takes over and you become someone you no longer recognize. Your eating disorder becomes more important to you than your values and beliefs because one of the lies we tell ourselves and grow to believe is that we cannot possibly function without the eating disorder and that we must do whatever we have to do in order to hold on to it.

It usually starts out by saying you have already eaten when you haven't or by telling someone you aren't eating because you don't feel well when you know that isn't true. At first, the lies bother you and you feel guilty but eventually you reach a point that they are so normal that you no longer think anything of them.

We lie about how we feel. An eating disorder is an unhealthy coping mechanism that is used to hide from uncomfortable emotions. The eating disorder provides a distraction and a mask to hide behind rather than dealing with whatever is really going on. One of the hardest parts of recovery, after you've dealt with and processed whatever it was that you were running from, is learning to continue being honest with your emotions because falling back into the lies can be such an easy stumbling block that is merely a gateway for falling headfirst back into the chains of your eating disorder. You have to learn to be honest with yourself and others about your emotions while learning how to appropriately express them and use healthy coping skills.

For myself, I used starvation and counting calories as a distraction and a coping mechanism to deal with sexual trauma, and then later the trauma of losing my son.

Then, an eating disorder lies to you. The worst part about that is, you hear the lies for so long that you believe them, and once you start to believe them, they go from being lies to your truths. Once they go from a lie to a truth that you wholeheartedly believe, they take roots and quickly grow like weeds taking over a garden and suffocating all of the beauty that had always called the garden home.

"You will never be good enough."

"No one cares about you. Look at you. You are a total failure. How could they?"

"You'll never do anything right. You will just continue to disappoint people."

"You could never be beautiful."

"You can't fix being a failure, but you can succeed with your eating disorder. At least you have that."

Do any of these lies sound familiar to you? If you have an eating disorder or have ever struggled with an eating disorder, they most likely resonate with something that your eating disorder has led you to believe. If you are reading this because a loved one is struggling or just to educate yourself, please know that this is only the *tiniest* peek into the mind of someone with an eating disorder. Take that dialogue and multiply it times every single moment that you are awake every single day and add hundreds more similarly strong statements that foster self-hatred. Then you might have a small idea of what someone is struggling with.

But my dearest friend reading this book, if you are the one struggling or who has struggled, these are lies. Lies. If you are reading this because you are desperate to help a loved one or if you are simply reading it for education about eating disorders, the chains that these lies form around a person can be broken.

The weed that is an eating disorder can grow so deeply within a person that it takes over and no matter how many times they seek treatment and no matter how many different types of treatment and different places they seek treatment, it comes back. The bystanders who love the beautiful garden feel helpless every time they see it starting to peek back through the beautiful blossoms.

Eventually, the weeds turn to chains and at times, they do seem permanent and impenetrable. Those longing to help become so frustrated and feel so helpless that they give up. Sometimes they lash out in frustration at the person bound by the chains because they just don't know what else to do.

The person trapped in the chains feels so weighed down and heavy that they don't even feel like they have the energy to stand, much less fight. They can see the frustration of those around them and they become even more frustrated as well which only feeds those lies that the eating disorder is telling them.

But friend, I have some good news. There is no lie that your eating disorder can tell that the truth of Jesus cannot destroy. There is no weed that His loving arms cannot remove from your beautiful, blossoming heart. There is no weight that He will not bear for you if you allow Him to. There is no chain that He cannot break, allowing you to run, holding them above your head in His victory.

The Lord will fight for you; you need only to be still.
   Exodus 14:14 (NIV)

You shall not fear them, for it is the Lord your God who fights for you.

Deuteronomy 3:22 (ESV)

Let Him. I know how easy that sounds. I also know how hard it is to actually let go of that control that you think your eating disorder gives you. I sat in those same shoes many a night with part of me longing to hand over the struggle and be done with it while the other part of me shook in terror at the thought of not having control over my food and what went into my body. I am all too familiar with the weight of living with an eating disorder, and I am blessed to know the freedom and peace that comes when the side of you that is desperate to be still finally wins and surrenders. I am blessed to know the peace that only Jesus can give when you let Him fight for you. It's so worth it. Choose peace.

He wants to fight for you.

Let Him.

CHAPTER 4
SURRENDER ISN'T EASY

I can feel the fibers of the bathroom rug digging into my knees as I sit folded over them, prostrate, on the floor. The cold ceramic tiles are pressed against my toes that hang off of the rug. Surrounding me on the walls are Bible verses and affirmations that I posted as daily reminders of God's love for me and His plan for my life, hoping that one day I could truly hold on to them.

I sniff a horrible ugly crying sniff as I raise my head and grab my phone. Music begins to play from my phone after I tell it to play on shuffle and "Jesus music", as my oldest daughter calls it, filled the space of that small bathroom that I shared with my precious roommate at A Center for Eating Disorders.

I was "ugly crying", but for a beautiful reason. I think I said it best when the moment was fresh on my mind and I shared it on my blog:

Today, my heart is overwhelmed. My mind envisions the scene on How the Grinch Stole Christmas (the original cartoon version) when the heart of the Grinch swells so big that the box it was contained in at the beginning can no longer hold all the joy that is within it when the Grinch discovers life and connections outside of his mountain top cave.

Two words have defined my life this week: But God.

I'm struggling with this today, *but God* intimately

knows my struggles.

I'm not sure I can do this, *but God* tells me in Philippians 4:13 that with Him, I can.

I'm so tired of fighting this battle, *but God* promises that He will fight for me.

I am so afraid, *but God* assures that He grants strength and courage.

I don't like myself today, *but God* says I am fearfully and wonderfully made in His image.

I can't take anymore today, *but God* promises shelter like no other.

I don't understand why I have to deal with this, *but God* promises to work all things together for good for those who love Him.

    The list goes on and on. Last week during my quiet time one morning, I felt so broken. Treatment for my eating disorder has been, is, and will continue to be hard work. It's emotionally, physically, and mentally draining. But it's exactly where I'm supposed to be and I have no doubt that it has all been God orchestrated.

I think back to when I first came to treatment, and I don't know where that person is anymore. She was cowering in the corner covering her face, trapped there by fear, insecurities, doubt, shame, and guilt. The chains that were so intricately linked together weighed more than she did. She knew she needed help, but to her that felt like admitting failure. She knew she needed help, because she finally realized that she didn't know how to help herself and she was suffocating in the small, dark corner that had become her entire world.

She tried to save herself by staying busy and trying to do "good" things by giving her time and her love away constantly by serving others. And she gave and she gave and she gave, but she never truly received anything sent back her way because she felt undeserving and unworthy. One day, she had no more to give. She realized that she was empty.

Humbled, she realized that she once again found herself in a situation where she had to release her stubborn grip from the control that she thought that she had, and she had to hand over all that she had left to God. All that she had to give Him was herself and the mess she had made of herself, and that was enough. God could work with that. She knew that logically, but she didn't truly believe it yet. She thought that she was too broken.

God took her and uprooted her. She was obedient, but not accepting. She knew that she needed help from the people that God placed in her path, but she resisted. This eating disorder, the pain and trauma, the guilt and shame and fear and doubts and insecurities were all she knew anymore. Who would she be without them? What would occupy her mind without them? Could she really loosen her grip in order to discover the key to the chains?

She decided to try, but she was stubborn. In order to loosen the grip, she would have to experience emotions that she didn't want to feel.

She would have to experience emotions that she had shoved away for years. She would have to explore them in depth. She would have to cry and truly feel everything she had been afraid of feeling. She would have to start unpacking all of it bit by bit from the safe in which she locked them deep inside. She would be challenged and have to face things about herself that she didn't want to face. It would be hard, and she was afraid.

    Gradually the grip did start to loosen and I started to emerge from within her. I began to learn how to admit when I needed help and how to ask for it. I started learning that my eating disorder isn't about food, but rather, that food is an unhealthy way of coping that was forced on me by things in my past combined with my inability to process it all on my own and my stubbornness that held it inside of me for so long. I had to learn to start separating my emotions from the food. I'm still learning these skills. I'm a work in progress. I have to continue to get to know who I really am.

    But on that day during that quiet time, God

was speaking to me and for once, I was quiet enough to hear.

And I could feel God telling me: **"Lay it down. I see that you are tired. I see that you're going to continue breaking if you keep trying to do this alone. Let me fight for you"**.

But I argued: "*God I have tried that so many times with this eating disorder and all of this other stuff, but it hasn't worked. It would only work for a short amount of time and then I was back in that downward spiral*".

God: **Have you truly ever laid it down?**

Me: *Yes! So many times I have tried!*

God: **How did you try?**

Me: *Well I've...I've taken it to the cross and laid it at your feet. But then, I picked it up and took it back with me over and over again. There isn't a try. It's either left at Your feet or it isn't.*

And in that moment I did break, but I broke in the way that I have needed to break for so long. Suddenly, that girl in the corner lifted her head. And she stood. The chains fell to the ground. She had realized that truly laying it down doesn't mean that she would be instantly healed. She accepted that there was still a long road of hard work ahead, and that is ok. As she turned to look and take in the world around her that she had hid from for so long, a little sparkle shone from her eye and a little confidence entered her step. And in that moment, I realized that the entire time, I've been staring into a mirror.

That sparkle was in my own eye. The bit of confidence was within my own steps, and I no longer saw a frightened and trapped girl, but rather a young woman who realized that the world outside of her eating disorder and disordered thoughts was a big, beautiful world full of joyful moments with herself and other people waiting to happen. And it was scary. But it wasn't the same fear that kept her trapped in the corner. This scary...it was exciting; it was an adrenaline rush. She craved more. She craved more Jesus. She craved more genuine connections with other people. She craved adventure and the chances to take in the beauty of this world and the people in it.

"God, what do I do next? How do I get there?"

"Trust. Trust in me. Trust the recovery process. Trust yourself. Just trust."

And as I begin to trust, I am finding joy everywhere. There is joy in seeing another person take a huge step forward. There is joy in the smiles at the nursing home while you sing unrehearsed Christmas carols. There is joy when I look at all of God's creation through a camera lens. There is joy when I sit down with a paintbrush or a pencil. There is joy in smashing plates against a wall. There is joy in serving Christ. There is joy in practicing self-care. There is joy in serving and loving others. To love and give, you must also be willing to give God His time first, and take time for yourself also.

There is joy in discovering what really sets your soul on fire and being passionate in your pursuit of that. There is joy in feeling at peace with where you are and where you've come from, and where you still have to travel. There is joy in God orchestrated moments that result in having church with a complete stranger in an aisle at Target. There is joy in obedience when He calls you to serve, but then also gently reminds you to balance it with the right amount of self care; refilling so that you can come back and serve and experience the true joy of giving.

We focus so much on what is wrong in this world. But today I can say with confidence that there is so much joy to be found. You just have to seek it. For me, that is seeking God first and the joy comes automatically.

I can't claim recovery yet. It's still the flag at the top of Mount Everest that sometimes seems farther away than others. But I'm still climbing. I'm not giving up. I am accepting that the climb will be hard and that there will be times that I stumble or feel like quitting. But I am trusting.

For the first time I am truly experiencing joy and the life that God has had planned for me all along; true, undeniable, joy.

He is so good.

Jesus paid it all,

All to Him I owe.

Seven months later, I found myself in an ice cream parlor, worrying only over what type of cone would go best with the flavor I had chosen, smiling at my husband, and giggling as our toddler got more ice cream on her face than in her mouth. Surrendering to Jesus changed my life.

In the beginning stages of my struggle with anorexia, I had a skewed view of what it meant to surrender the battle to God. I thought that if I walked an aisle when I felt God speaking to me, if I prayed an eloquent prayer of surrender, or if I allowed my fellow believers to pray over me and my struggle, then I would stand up and walk away free from the bondage of anorexia and that would be the end of that struggle.

Here's a hint: *It's not that easy.* Or, at least, it

wasn't that easy for me.

Several aisles were walked and I lost count of how many pews I soaked in my tears as I cried and told God that I was done and that I was ready to hand it all over to Him. That was partly true. I was really, *really* tired. This daily fight wore me down to complete exhaustion by early morning on a daily basis, both physically and emotionally. However, as much as I believed I was ready to hand it over to God, I wasn't quite there. I wanted God to fix me, but I didn't want to actually do any of the work I needed to do for that healing process to take place and I was too afraid to trust God to provide for me everything that I thought my eating disorder provided for me.

It wasn't until I was four months into the recovery process that I realized the pattern I had been following with God. I would walk the aisle or kneel at a pew, and I would take the struggle that was my eating disorder, and I would absolutely lay it down at the cross, at the feet of Jesus. I would end my heartfelt prayer, and as I stood to return to my seat or to join back in the worship song being played, I would reach down and pick it right back up, clinging to it just as tightly as I had before I momentarily laid it down.

I was doing it all wrong.

It was in the midst of crying out to God and arguing with God that I finally realized the problem with how I was confronting the presence of anorexia in my life.

"God, I'm SO tired of this battle. I'm exhausted in every way. I need some rest. I want this to be over."

"Give it to Me."

"God, I have! So many times I have given this struggle to You, yet here I am and it's just as bad as ever."

"Have you really given it to Me?"

"Yes, Lord. You know I have. I've given it to you so many times, but..."

And in that last three letter word, I realized so much. Yes, I had laid it down so many times, but the problem is that when it comes to truly handing something over to God, there is no "but". You either hand it over completely to Him or you don't. I was laying it down on an altar, but as soon as I stood to walk back to my seat, I was gathering it back up like a security blanket that I thought I couldn't live without. It was a halfhearted surrender.

Cast your burden on the Lord, and He will sustain you; He will never permit the righteous to be moved.
Psalm 55:22 (ESV)

Casting all your anxieties on Him, because He cares for you.
1 Peter 5:7 (ESV)

If you're like I was in the midst of my eating disorder and part of what holds you back from handing this battle over to the Lord is because you think you are a burden, let me tell you this right now: *that is a lie straight from the pit.*

God created you to have a relationship with Him and He longs to be involved in every single detail, big and small, of your life. He never has and never will view you as a burden, but instead, sees you as His precious child.

See what great love the Father has lavished on us, that we should be called children of God!
1 John 3:1 (NIV)

The thing about surrender that I didn't fully understand until the day God opened my eyes to my halfhearted surrender is that surrender doesn't mean it is instantly over. My eating disorder didn't end the moment I handed it over to God, although I know that He could have done that if He chose to. However, God had a lot to teach me within the trenches of the battle against this disorder that had consumed so much of my life. In order to learn those lessons, God needed me to tie up the laces of my boots and wade deep down into that nasty muck.

My eating disorder didn't end in that moment, but I no longer felt the heavy load of a burden that had always been far more than I could carry. I had a heavenly Father walking alongside me carrying the load and waiting with open arms to embrace me when the recovery process felt overwhelming and I needed to fall in

His arms and rest awhile.

Wholehearted surrender to Jesus will radically transform your life, whether you are surrendering your life to Him for the first time, surrendering a struggle with an eating disorder, or whatever else He may be calling you to surrender to Him. Just know that continuing to struggle after surrendering doesn't mean you failed or that God doesn't care; it just means that God is still working in you and teaching you something, but He is right there, carrying the load, and waiting to wrap you up in His loving arms as soon as you ask for His rest and embrace.

He loves you...*wholeheartedly.*

CHAPTER 5
GIRL LOST

The branches of a large oak tree sway in the wind blowing outside as I refuse to break my stare out the window opposite of where I am sitting. My arms are folded firmly across my chest and my legs bob quickly up and down as I try diligently to wish the day away.

I'm angry, but I don't know with whom or what. In my mind, a battle wages on. I want to recover. I want to get out of treatment and return to normal life.

But I am afraid, and that makes me angry. I am afraid of who I will be if I recover. I am afraid of what life in recovery will be like. I am afraid of failure.

My stare is broken as I uncross my arms and stand up from the soft beige couch on which I was sitting. I make my way out of the room and down the hall to the door that leads to the back porch. I need fresh air.

I climb onto the back porch swing and as the breeze crosses my face, tears sneak out of the corner of each eye. My fear was creeping out of the corner of the eyes and running down my cheeks. I quickly wiped them away with my sleeve and shoved the headphones of my iPod in my ears, drowning out my own thoughts.

I was afraid. I was confused. I was tired.

One of my greatest fears about surrendering my eating disorder fully to the Lord was the fear of losing myself. For so long my identity had been wrapped up in my eating disorder. I was "the skinny girl" and "the girl who never ate". For years my days were consumed by counting and tracking calories, weighing myself multiple times a day, over exercising, body checking, and critiquing myself that I was terrified that I wouldn't know what to do or who I was without my eating disorder. What I didn't yet realize was that I had lost myself to the eating disorder a long time ago and I already didn't know who I was. Anorexia was all that I knew, and it was no way to live.

My eating disorder almost took everything from me, but the only things that I could see were the things that it gave me. Anorexia gave me a sense of control. Being raped when I was sixteen launched a spiral that would continue to be set off through the years and it made me feel like my life was completely out of control. That man made me feel like I didn't even have control over my own body, and in the aftermath, that was something that I desperately needed.

The problem was that the control that I thought my eating disorder restored to me was completely false. Sure, I had some control over my body in the beginning. I controlled exactly what went into my body. It never occurred to me that I was actually losing even more control at a very rapid pace.

I can still remember the moment that I realized that I no longer controlled what my body ate, but that my eating disorder now controlled me as well. I decided that I was done with my eating disorder. I was tired of starving myself and counting calories. I was exhausted from never having energy and trying to keep up with my fast paced high school life. I was done with my eating disorder and I was going to just start eating and be "normal" again.

When I found myself in a stall in the girls' bathroom at school forcing myself to vomit after eating lunch in the cafeteria, I panicked as I realized that I no longer had any control over this aspect of my life. Eating one complete meal had sent me into such a panic that I thought I would surely perish if I did not find a way to purge the food from my body. The terror I felt as I realized what I had just done only grew as I realized that I actually felt relieved once the food was no longer inside of me. I no longer had an eating disorder. The eating disorder had me.

Anorexia became like that friend that is a negative, draining relationship that you can't seem to let go of because it's comfortable and familiar. No matter how many times I tried to end the relationship, I would quickly go running back in order to avoid the panic that would sweep over me. This continued until my entire identity rested solely in the eating disorder. I no longer knew anything about who I was, what I valued, or who I wanted to become. I was lost.

When I entered treatment for the last time, knowing that this had to be the time that I found healing somehow, I felt that same panic slipping up as I thought of surrendering the identity that had consumed a decade of my life. I was terrified of actually having to figure out who I really was and who I wanted to become. That would mean I would have to actually face the reasons behind the eating disorder and that was my greatest fear. Anorexia helped me avoid those demons. Recovery would mean facing them and working through them.

But to all who did receive Him, who believed in His name, He gave the right to become children of God.
John 1:12 (ESV)

Facing this fear was a huge turning point for me in the recovery process and the courage to face that fear came from the truth found in John

1:12. As a Christian who had accepted Jesus as my Savior, I already had a rock solid identity in Christ. The work was going to be exploring that identity in Christ, acknowledging it, and believing it with every single ounce of my being. Being active in my church and Sunday School class was pivotal in helping me to explore the different components of my identity in Christ and being reminded of those truths on a consistent basis.

I am His daughter. I have received Him as my Savior and believe that He is Lord of all. He calls me His daughter. If you are a believer, the same is true for you. If you haven't accepted Him, you have the opportunity to do so. Think about this for just a second; the God of *everything* chooses to call you His beloved child. This relationship affords you everything that a parent child relationship has to offer, only this particular relationship involves a perfect Father. If you're feeling overwhelmed, read John 1:12 and climb into His arms for a while. You will find rest in His embrace that only He can give. He longs to have that Father-child relationship with you.

I am His unique craftsmanship whom He carefully designed and created. I am beautiful.

Psalm 139 beautifully details how God knew every detail of our lives well before we were ever thought of or formed within our mother's womb. We are fearfully and wonderfully made *in His image*. I fully understand that this one can be a hard one to grasp. Casting aside the world's definition of beauty, the definition that we have been taught to cling to as truth, and developing your own definition of beauty by viewing everyone as a unique piece of art formed by our Creator is no easy task. Don't try to complete this transformation on your own. Ask God for His eyes to see not only yourself, but every individual who crosses your path, as a unique and beautiful piece of art uniquely inspired by God.

I am known. You are understood. The pain you are feeling, the exhaustion, the desperation, the stress, the aching; He knows. He knows exactly how all of it feels. No one else can fully know and understand you like Jesus can. Humans are relational beings and we all desperately seek to be understood by someone. When you have a relationship with Jesus, you need not look far. He is always available.

I am treasured. In Matthew 10:29-31, God reminds us that not even a sparrow goes unnoticed by the Father and every hair on your head is numbered, yet our value in His eyes is so much more than many sparrows. As the hymn says, *His eye is on the sparrow and I know He watches me*. Let this actually sink in. God, who created the universe and every living thing within it, sees every moment of every life that ever takes a breath on this earth. He sees you. He *cares* about you. He knows your every thought, hurt, joy, smile, and tear. He created you in His image and He adores and treasures you.

I am infinitely and intimately loved. God, Abba Father, loves me unconditionally. He knows me more intimately than myself or anyone else ever could, flaws and all, yet He loves me unconditionally for all of eternity. His love is a mind boggling, odd-defying, radical love.

That radical love never falters.

It is never altered.

It is never lessened or weakened.

It never fails.

CHAPTER 6
PICKING GRAPES

"What is one thing you like about your body?"

Easy. Nothing.

That was always my answer. I never had to think about it. I never needed time to ponder. If I was forced to come up with an answer, it was always, "that it carried my children". While true, in my mind I wanted to add about how my stretch marks bothered me and how I hated that little bit of my stomach that would never quite go back to where it was before my children.

On the contrary, if you had asked me, before recovery, what I hated about my body, I could have easily listed off a hundred answers.

Anorexia had consumed my life and my thoughts to the point that I could no longer see myself as God's creation. The beautiful truth of being fearfully and wonderfully made in His image was overshadowed by the dark cloud of an eating disorder.

I picked up a marker and carefully drew what I believed my body to look like. I made sure to capture every perceived flaw that in my mind affected the outline of this vessel I inhabited.

Then, I took a moment to lie on another piece of paper while someone else traced the actual outline of my body and I was forced to face the differences and the skewed view that I held. The problem was that when I first completed this exercise, my first thoughts were not about the false views I had of my body. My immediate thoughts were that there must be a mistake with the tracing because that was NOT my body.

Angrily, I walked away from the exercise and no longer wanted to participate, convinced that I was being lied to by the people around me instead of facing the truth that I was being lied to by the disorder that had stolen my life.

It would be months before I could revisit that exercise and see the truth behind it.

Recently I was in my kitchen washing some grapes that I had just purchased and placing the clean ones into a plastic container to put back in the refrigerator. As I was washing the grapes, I would look them over and toss aside the ones that were "mushy" or had gaping holes or bruises amongst their purple skin. About halfway through this process, God reminded me of how I would previously sit in front of my mirror looking myself over and picking out all of my flaws and the gratitude that that is no longer my life was overwhelming.

I paused as I held a grape in my hand that was beginning to lose its firmness, yet wasn't quite to the point that I would automatically toss it. As I rolled it around in my hand, I debated on whether I should toss it or keep it. Eventually I ate it and the sweetest taste filled my mouth as the juice from the grape erupted from beneath its skin. That delicious grape was almost tossed in the trash can.

I began to wonder what it would be like if we were able to pick through life in the same way that I was picking through the grapes. What flaws would we consider severe enough to toss aside and which ones would be tolerable? It was just a grape, but I couldn't help but think about the grapes that I had just eaten but had almost tossed into the trash. Do we miss out on beautiful things in life because we reject something tiny that we consider to be a flaw? How many times is perceived beauty actually disguising a sour grape?

Would I toss my freckles that remind me of too much time spent in the sun as a teenager? Would I trade the breakouts that still plague my face one week a month (getting personal here!)? The interesting thing is that as I am writing this I had to work kind of hard to come up with those two examples. It's not because I have some high opinion of myself, but that God has taught me to see beauty in what I formerly viewed as eternal flaws. I love my freckles and, though I don't love the once a month breakout on my face, I can handle a little bit of concealer. When I was in my eating disorder, I could have filled this entire book with things that I would change about myself.

The freckles on my face remind me of fun summer days lying in the sun with a dear friend with our favorite music blasting from the speakers of a CD player spinning a mixed CD that we had just burned on the computer. The stretch marks on my stomach remind me of that beautiful gift that carrying my children was and what a privilege that is. Scars remind me of what healing means. Every day, every moment, is a gift that I am able to love and enjoy because God has blessed me with a body that enables me to participate and be present.

This wasn't always how I felt and it took a lot of work on my part, and a radical healing from God to get to this point. Previously, I despised every part of my body. The reasons we hate our body can vary depending on what triggered the eating disorder, but a common thread among eating disorders is disliking your body. For me, when I saw my body, I replayed the night that I was raped. What I perceived as flaws were all things that, if I could change them, if I could take back some semblance of control, then it would never happen to me again. That was my line of thinking. As flawed as that reasoning was, it was the only thing about myself that I didn't see as a flaw.

I always hated when people would tell me that I just needed to be grateful, so that is the last piece of advice that I am going to sit here and write down for you. An attitude of gratitude is an amazing tool, but I also believe that in order to possess an attitude of gratitude, you must first have a genuine appreciation. Genuine appreciation grows from realizing your own value and when you have an eating disorder, that can be one of the hardest obstacles to overcome.

Take a pack of sticky notes, or notecards, or whatever you have handy and sit down with them and a pen. Instead of picking out your flaws as the grapes reminded me that I formerly did, think of things that you like about yourself. If physical attributes are more difficult, start with something else. Even on my darkest days, I could always find one positive thing about myself; I was passionate. I clung to that attribute. When I believed nothing else positive about myself, I knew that I was passionate about anything I set my mind to.

For each positive attribute that you believe about yourself, even if not quite wholeheartedly, write it down on a sticky note or notecard. If you enjoy art or doodling, dress them up. When you are finished, take what you have, even if you start with just one, and stick them somewhere that you will pass by each day. At one point I had them in my journal, then my bathroom mirror, and then I moved them to my closet. Look at this group of attributes every day and read them each time that you pass them. Speak them out loud. Add to them when another comes to mind. When you don't believe them, speak them anyway.

I had a hard time with this for so long because I still had that skewed view of humility and I thought that this was essentially bragging and a terrible thing to do. It's not. Finding positive things about yourself and speaking them and believing them is acknowledging God's goodness and expressing gratitude for His blessings and provision and that is a beautiful thing.

If you view yourself as a piece of art, a canvas that an artist has spent much time pouring love and work into, it helps to change how you view this practice. You wouldn't stand in front of that piece of art and pick out every perceived flaw and go on and on about each one of them to the artist who poured so much time and love into the piece. Why do we do that to God?

So God created man in His own image, in the image of God He created him; male and female He created them.
Genesis 1:27 (ESV)

CHAPTER 7
FEAR

The end of my finger started to go numb as I tightly wound a thread from my sweatpants around it, desperately trying to pass the time. I unwound the thread and immediately starting winding it back around, repeating this process over and over again.

Around me, voices fill the air as everyone else

participates in group therapy, but I can only hear them. I am afraid of talking; afraid of revealing anything about myself to these people I have just met, so I sit in the corner, curled in a ball, a soft red blanket covering my face.

I know it's silly and it's not helping me, but I am afraid. If these people see who I really am, they will run. If they know why I stopped eating, they'll never look back. If they see how broken I really am, they will run faster. So I hide, hoping to prevent their departure.

Do people really run? Or do I push them away in fear? In this moment, I was sure that they ran.

At dinner, I eat my food as fast as I can. I don't want a supplement, but I don't want to taste my food or give myself time to think about what I am eating. I sit in silence, ignoring the conversation around me, and retreating into my own mind. I am afraid to venture out.

After dinner, I help with dishes and then retreat to my room, afraid of true connections. Some form of fear drives every decision that I make. But this is my normal.

Fear consumed years of my life. The main reason that anorexia raged in my life and that I so desperately sought control over something in my life was because I lived in complete fear. I feared being hurt again. I feared being put in a position in which I did not have control over my own body again. I was afraid of people, I was afraid of not being able to protect myself, and I was afraid of life.

I carried fear around like Linus carried his beloved blanket around in Charles Schulz's *Peanuts*. The gravity of fear's presence in my life and the weight of it has it held me down were obvious, but in my mind, to release the fear meant taking off my armor and allowing myself to be vulnerable. Vulnerability carried its own new set of fears.

There was nothing I feared more than vulnerability and I don't know that the fear of vulnerability ever completely goes away, but it can be quieted from the megaphone in your ear to a faint whisper that is more easily surpassed.

Have I not commanded you? Be strong and

courageous. Do not be afraid; do not be discouraged, for the Lord your God will be with you wherever you go.
    Joshua 1:9 (NIV)

    I carry this verse with me every moment of my life. God reminds us that fear is unnecessary. It is a weight that we don't have to carry and a burden that we don't have to bear. In saying that, I also understand the fear of releasing your fear.

    After a period of time, fear begins to feel like a shield or a wall of protection that keeps you safe. Fear feels like a safety barrier that constantly has you on alert and prevents you from missing something that you might not notice if your senses weren't on high alert with your heightened fear. Your mind begins to tell you that if you surrender your fear, you will get hurt.

    The thing is, holding on to your fear is going to hurt you. Holding on to your fear causes you to constantly replay and relive whatever it is that you are afraid of.

    One day, after letting something a random

person said to me take over my entire day because it ignited that fear that I carry so closely, I was forced to examine what exactly it was that I was gaining from holding on so tightly to that fear. It was only when my list came up short that I began to see everything that fear was taking away from me. I had missed out on an entire day, missed out on personal growth and laughter with friends, because one thing that a stranger said to me in passing was enough to set that fear ablaze.

Fear was not protecting me. Fear was hindering me.

To a certain degree we do need fear. Healthy fear keeps us appropriately aware of our surroundings and keeps us from doing participating in reckless activities. However, when fear crosses the boundary between being that first aid kit we keep in the trunk to being in the driver's seat, it is no longer doing its job and it is unqualified for the position it has taken over.

Fear tends to have a prominent place in an eating disorder. Fear ranges from a fear of gaining weight, to a fear of failure, or a fear of not being good enough, or a fear of being hurt or traumas repeating themselves, and the list goes on and on and on.

This may be the only chapter in this book that bears the title of fear, but if you look, every single one can be traced back to a fear of something. Fear sat in my driver's seat for far too long.
What does God say about fear?

Peace I live with you; My peace I give to you. Not as the world gives do I give to you. Let not your hearts be troubled, neither let them be afraid.
John 14:27 (ESV)

Therefore, do not be anxious about tomorrow, for tomorrow will be anxious for itself. Sufficient for the day is its own trouble.
Matthew 6:24 (ESV)

But now thus says the Lord, He who created you, O Jacob, He who formed you, O Israel; "Fear not, for I have redeemed you; I have called you by name, you are mine."
Isaiah 43:1 (ESV)

That last one gives me chills. He calls us by name. We are treasured and precious in His sight. He knows and He understands. He sees and He cares.

"When you pass through the waters, I will be with you; and through the rivers, they shall not overwhelm you; when you walk through fire you shall not be burned, and the flame shall not consume you."
Isaiah 43:2 (ESV)

We need not fear, because we are never alone. The God who moves mountains, He is on your side, and He walks with you.

What are you afraid of today? What fear are you clinging to? Is it in the driver's seat? Give it to God, wholly and completely. Put it back where it belongs. Cling to His love and provision instead.

CHAPTER 8
BREAKING DOWN WALLS

The intricately stacked stones stand in solidarity as my eyes move from top to bottom and side-to-side, trying to decide where I should start. Do I try to climb? Do I search for a gap that I can squeeze through? I'm not certain, but I do know that the wall has got to go.

You see, I have been stuck at this same spot facing this same wall for ten years now. Every situation and every emotion that I try to deal with by silence and starving myself only adds another stone. This has carried on until the wall seemed impossible to overcome.

But now, I have the help and the tools that I

have needed all along to get past it. The problem is, I am afraid. I want to climb the wall. I want to use the strength I have to climb it stone by stone to the very top and claim victory upon reaching the other side. I want to find a gap in the stones big enough to squeeze through and make a quick trip to the other side.

What I don't want to do is dismantle the wall. Dismantling the wall means facing every single stone and the hurt that comes with it. Breaking this wall down means lots of hurt, lots of tears, and a lot of work. But deep down, I know that the only way to claim that victory on the other side is to tear it down, solid rock by solid rock, piece by piece, hurt by hurt, silenced emotion by silenced emotion.

The problem with climbing to the top is that you have to find a way to get down on the other side once you reach the top, and I would probably plummet to the ground. The problem with finding a gap to squeeze through is the risk of getting stuck and finding myself once again trapped in the same place, only this time with the load of all of those stones on my shoulders. Yes, the only way was to tear it down and walk right across the rubble to claim the victory awaiting me on the other side.

It's time to do this. I look down at my tool belt: supportive professionals and friends, supportive friends and family, coping skills, church family, and the Master tool, my Jesus.

With Your help I can advance against a troop; with my God I can scale a wall.
Psalm 18:29 (NIV)

A few months in treatment passed before I really got a grasp on what it would take to achieve recovery. I think I started out believing that if I did what I was supposed to do, followed all the rules, saw a therapist, went to group, and ate what I was supposed to eat, then I would get better. That, in and of itself, was hard enough. Those chalky supplements made more appearances in my life during treatment than I wanted because I simply could not finish a meal.

I had no problem telling my story and the trauma that led to the development of my eating disorder. I stood in front of the staff and my peers at treatment one of my first weeks there and very speedily recapped what brought me there without shedding the first tear. I had learned to do that. I told the story like it happened to someone else, because if I cried, if I showed how much it hurt me, then I thought that showed weakness. The intense desire to protect myself told me that I could never show any perceived weaknesses.

I shifted in my seat on the couch uncomfortably as people asked me questions about my life story I had just told and when others cried for me, I wanted to leave the room.

One of the hardest parts of defeating an eating disorder is honestly facing everything that started it all. You have to face your past. And in facing your past, you also have to honestly face yourself.

Facing my past was hard enough. Admitting how much I was hurt by my past was more than I wanted to do. Working through that hurt, anger, fear, and every other emotion I can think of was way more than I imagined when I first entered treatment.

However, the hardest part for me was truly facing myself and admitting where I was allowing my eating disorder to win in my life even as I was working my way towards recovery. I had to admit when I wasn't asking for what I needed and then learn to do that. I had to admit when I was giving my eating disorder control, thereby admitting that I didn't have control, which was my biggest fear.

Getting to the root of an eating disorder is hard work, even if you know exactly what it was that triggered it. You still have to go back to that moment and unpack all of the emotions that you kept tucked away, hidden in that moving box in the garage. Unpacking them means feeling them, and feeling them is what the eating disorder helps you to avoid.

It will feel terrifying. At times, it will feel impossible. You will want to give up. Anger will fear you and you will begrudgingly admit that the anger is a result of fear.

But hold on, love. Don't give up. Don't listen to anyone, including yourself, that makes you feel like living with your eating disorder would be easier or better than going through it. Call them the lies that they are.

Strap on your helmet, and lace up your boots. Pick up your sword and your shield, and get ready to fight. You may not even believe it yet, but you are fighting for a cause that is beyond worthy.

You are fighting for *you*.

You are a beautiful child of God, fearfully and wonderfully made in the image and likeness of a creator who humbled Himself and walked among us, and then bore our sins and died *just to be with us. Just to be with you.*

You are beautiful.
You are treasured.

You are worthy.

You are brave.

You are fierce.

You are unique and precious.

You are loved.

You are His.

You are worth every moment of this battle. Don't you ever give up. Fight for you.

But here is the hard truth, friend: You **cannot** do this alone.

See what great love the Father has lavished on us, that we should be called children of God!
1 John 3:1 (NIV)

CHAPTER 9
ONLY JESUS

I do not want to be here right now and I am so ready for this day to be over.

That's how I feel on this night of treatment as dinner is creeping up. This day has seemed to drag on for forever and the absolute last thing that I want to do right now is eat AGAIN.

Even worse, on this particular night, dinner is family style, and even though I don't have kitchen privileges at dinner yet, I have to prepare my own plate. While I hate to be waited on here, I also hate having to put food on my own plate. I am terrified that I will put more than I am required to eat on my plate and being in the kitchen with so many people makes my anxiety shoot through the roof.

The door to the kitchen opens for someone to let us know that it's time to start preparing our plates. My arms fold across my chest and I turn to look out the window into the not quite dark yet evening sky, postponing the inevitable.

I don't want to be here tonight. I want to be at home with my husband and kids where no one tells me that I have to eat or go to a residential facility. I want to go back to life and not have to talk about my feelings. I want to run away. But I know I can't do that.

Eventually, I hear my name. Everyone else is already in the kitchen scooping food onto plates, hating it just as much as I do for the most part. I grab my plate, and as I walk to the kitchen, someone comes out and I see her plate.

Dinner is tacos.

And in that particular moment, it was absolutely more than I could take. By the time the sound of my plastic plate clattering on the tile floor of the kitchen reaches my ears, the front door is in my sight.

Running away sounds appealing, but I have no intention of doing that. I know I can't. But I desperately need fresh air.

The cool fall air greets my cheeks as I swing the front door open, and as I reach the brick steps leading to the front door and have a seat, I fall apart. The tears flow down my face like a raging body of water that has just breached a dam. I cover my face with the sleeves of my navy blue oversized sweatshirt, desperately trying to hide my brokenness.

On that porch, though a staff member soon joined me, I realized how alone I felt, and that I had felt that loneliness for a long time.

That night taught me a lot about the loneliness that I felt. I learned that loneliness can be felt no matter how many people you are surrounded by. I learned that for myself, I brought the loneliness on.

In order to keep my eating disorder in my life, I had pushed others out of my life.

Sure, if you followed me on Facebook or Instagram, my life seemed peachy and I was always hanging out with someone. The problem was, at least in my half of the relationship, it was all surface. I never let anyone get past surface level to see the real me. Even the ones who knew my secrets and knew my demons, I never let them see how it affected me.

Because of that, I felt alone. I refused to open the door and allow anyone inside the pit with me.

Friends, it doesn't work like that. Recovery will never work like that.

Being vulnerable is scary.

But being vulnerable is beautiful.

I know you probably think I am crazy. I would have to. The last thing I wanted to be was vulnerable. Yet here I am writing a book that gives you a glimpse into my mind that was overcome by anorexia. When this book is published, everyone will know that I had an eating disorder. But it's beautiful. We heal when we share.

And they have conquered him by the blood of the Lamb and by the word of their testimony..." Revelation 12:11 (ESV)

I began to heal when I began to allow myself to be vulnerable. Being vulnerable doesn't mean that you have to tell the world your struggle, or write a book to let everyone know. But you have to tell someone.

You need to talk to a professional.

You need the support of family and/or friends (depending on what's healthy in your situation).

Having support in church is amazing too if you have someone in your church you can talk to.

The important thing is that you can't keep it all inside.

The loneliness will smother you.

When you don't talk to someone, it leaves only your eating disorder to talk to, and the eating disorder will win that narrative when there is no one to help you combat it and help you sort out the dialogue going on.

On the days, and in the moments, when you feel like you can't talk to anyone else, talk to Jesus. On the days when you have already spilled your guts and you're tired of talking, talk to Him anyway. Let Him walk alongside you in this journey and carry you when it becomes more than you can bear. You're a fighter, and you are in this battle to win it, but I know that there will be days when you are too tired to fight. That doesn't mean you give up. It means you fight harder by giving Him the reigns and letting the ultimate Victor fight for you.

The Lord will fight for you; you need only to be still.
Exodus 14:14 (NIV)

Jesus provides us with invaluable resources through professional treatment, and I encourage you to please take advantage of that and please seek professional treatment. But know this: you can't do it alone, and you can't do it with just treatment.

Jesus, only Jesus.

CHAPTER 10
THE VOICES WE HEAR

Worthless. Inadequate. Failure. Ugly. Fat.

I draw a teardrop at the top of my page and place my pen back down on the lunch table. I'm tired of writing my feelings down. After a meal like this, they are especially hard to face.

My eating disorder tells me that I am a failure and don't deserve to eat. Despite what medical professionals and measurements tell me, my eating disorder tells me I am huge. My eating disorder tells me that I have no control over my body when I eat and I am opening myself up to be hurt again.

My eating disorder tells me that everyone is lying to me and that these thoughts I am having are truth.

My eating disorder tells me that I serve no purpose and that I mess things up for myself and everyone else.

My eating disorder tells me that I am unworthy of anyone's love or time.

My eating disorder tells me that I am the reason I was raped at the age of 16.

My eating disorder tells me that I don't even deserve to be in treatment.

My eating disorder tells me that I don't deserve recovery and that I should run to the bathroom and get rid of the food that I am being forced to eat.

I look at my watch. Two minutes have passed. My eating disorder just told me all of that in two minutes.

One of the most painful parts of an eating disorder is that you cannot escape it.

My husband once told me that watching me struggle with anorexia was like watching someone slowly killing me and there was nothing he could do to stop it.

Looking back, he is absolutely right. An eating disorder is like having a bully slowly take your life from you. Only the bully lives inside your head, and the bully is you.

When speaking with my peers we would often refer to our "healthy voice" and our "eating disorder voice". At the beginning of an eating disorder, they start out as two separate beings and the person feels like they are in complete control. (Now these are thoughts, not literal voices.)

As the eating disorder progresses, the two begin to morph together until, at some point, it becomes nearly impossible for the person to separate the two.

Learning to separate the two inside my own

mind was a difficult hurdle to overcome. It was one that was only overcome by diving into His word.

The more time I spent reading my Bible, and the more time I spent in worship and prayer, the easier it was to differentiate between the two. Clearly the eating disorder thoughts did not align with what God says. Familiarity with God's word and what He says about His children allowed me to be able to recognize the lies that were constantly being thrown at me by the eating disorder.

The eating disorder told me I was weak.

I can do all things through Him who strengthens me.
Philippians 4:13 (ESV)

The eating disorder told me I was worthless.

Therefore I tell you, do not be anxious about your life, what you will eat or what you will drink, nor about your body, what you will put on. Is not life more than food, and the body more than clothing? Look at the birds of the air; they neither

sow nor reap nor gather into barns, and yet your heavenly Father feeds them. Are you not of more value than they?
  Matthew 6:25-26

The eating disorder told me I was inadequate.

But you are a chosen race, a royal priesthood, a holy nation, a people for His own possession, that you may proclaim the excellencies of Him who called you out of darkness into His marvelous light.
  1 Peter 2:9 (ESV)

The eating disorder told me that no one could ever truly love me because of my unworthiness.

This is how we know what love is: Jesus Christ laid down His life for us. And we ought to lay down our lives for our brothers and sisters.
  1 John 3:16 (NIV)

The eating disorder told me that I was alone and that no one understood what I was dealing with.

For we do not have a high priest who is unable

to sympathize with our weaknesses, but one who in every respect has been tempted as we are, yet without sin.
Hebrews 4:15 (ESV)

I could go on and one, but for every single lie that my eating disorder has ever told me, God had something different to say.

Here's what I finally realized: I could continue on claiming to be a follower of Christ and believing my eating disorder, or I could continue on as a follower of Christ believing what my Creator says about me.

I had to get honest with myself and realize that by choosing to believe my eating disorder over the Word of God that I was essentially calling Jesus a liar. That stung, and stepped on a lot more than just my toes.

Hear me out on this one. This is important. **Your eating disorder is NOT your fault**. It never has been and never will be. Despite what so many people think, an eating disorder is a disease, not a choice.

Your choice lies in what you choose to do with what God says about you. Was I able to make a radical turnaround over night of how I thought about myself? Not at all.

Finding confidence in my identity as a fearfully and wonderfully made, cherished daughter of the King took time and commitment on my part. It took immersing myself in His word so that when my eating disorder fed me those lies, I had truth to combat them with. It took writing scripture on notecards that I kept in my pocket to pull out when the voice of my eating disorder was overwhelming. It took plastering my walls in artwork that reminded me of His truths. It took scheduled and committed time in prayer, seeking an intimate relationship with my Heavenly Father.

And still, because I am human, because the enemy will attack, I still have days and moments where those thoughts try to creep back up. The difference is that they are no longer given any power.

CHAPTER 11
BREAKING PLATES

I had never felt anger like this before. Well, the anger had been there, but I had never allowed myself to really feel it.

Now, I wasn't so sure I wanted to feel it, but I knew I had to. Keeping it all locked inside was only hurting me. I was angry that someone had made a choice to hurt me and turn my life upside down. For the first time, I was allowing myself to be angry about the crime that was committed against my body and myself.

The only problem was that I didn't know how to let it out. I had been sitting with it all morning and I was exhausted.

Finally, I just said out loud "I am so angry that I just want to throw something. I want to throw something and let all of this out."

What I didn't expect was for the response from a friend telling me that that's exactly what I should do then. I had said it out loud, but the thought of actually doing it, of actually throwing something, hadn't really occurred to me. However, the more I thought about it, the more I really wanted to do it. I needed to do something symbolic.

Being angry might not seem like a big deal to most people, but it was for me. Being angry on this particular day for this particular reason was a sign that I was no longer placing the blame for what happened on myself. I was blaming the man who committed the crime against me. I needed to work through that in order to be able to forgive him.

So a dear soul that I will always treasure went with me to a local dollar store where I purchased ceramic plates in a variety of colors and one random ceramic mug for good measure. We took them back, and armed with gloves and safety glasses, I threw them as hard as I could against a brick wall.

Then, this sweet soul and I gathered up those tiny broken pieces and placed them all in a box where they would be taken to become an art project.

And oh did it work. I felt like a new person, and the joy that my Jesus had filled me with, spilled out on my face that day because the chains were breaking.

The chains of fear that bound me to slavery were being replaced with freedom, and it was something to smile about.

One thing that I realized about myself in treatment is that I had a lot of anger that I had let build up inside of myself. I had packed it away, never allowing myself to feel it because the lies that my eating disorder spewed from its ugly mouth made me believe that I had no right to be angry.

If it was my fault that I was raped, why would I have a right to be angry? The thing is I had every right to be angry and stuffing it deep inside myself only fueled my beliefs that I was to blame for the crime committed against my body.

The pictures of me throwing plates probably seem silly and insignificant to most people who have seen them, but for me, they will always symbolize a turning point. On that day, chains broke. The chains of self-blame and shame and doubt crumbled to the ground.

The smile on my face is not simply a smile of happiness, but a smile of joy.

You see, there is a big difference between the two and they are not at all interchangeable.

Happiness is circumstantial. Happiness can change in the blink of an eye. Happiness can disappear when you see a sad story on the news. Happiness runs away when a loved one dies. When life gets tough and you have to wade through the mud, happiness can be nowhere to be found.

Then there is joy. Joy is unwavering. It is not driven by your mood or your circumstances. Joy is a permanent fixture in the life of a follower of Christ. It cannot be removed, and it cannot be shaken.

Happiness is a feeling that we obtain from our circumstances.

Joy is a way of life gifted to us by our Savior.

You can be sad, hurt, happy, exhausted, disappointed, angry, etc., and still be full of joy.

These pictures of me throwing plates remind me of that. I was so angry, yet so full of joy.

I was so angry, and yet, the joy couldn't be contained and it spilled out and all over my face.

Friend, if you are spending your time searching this world for happiness, you are wasting it. Hear me again: you are wasting your time. Even if you find it, it will only be temporary.

What we truly seek is joy. It can't be found

in any treasure. Joy can't be found in a spouse or any other relationship. Joy cannot be found in material possessions. It can't be found in a job or a title.

Joy, true joy, can only be found in Jesus.

The search is over, friend.

May the God of hope fill you with all joy and peace as you trust in Him, so that you may overflow with hope by the power of the Holy Spirit.
Romans 15:13 (NIV)

CHAPTER 12
GET READY FOR BATTLE

An eating disorder is a daily fought battle. Recovery is something you have to fight for. It doesn't just come on its own and it doesn't come without hard work.

As a follower of Christ, you have the ultimate warrior waiting to go to battle for you. You only need to let Him fight for you.

You also have to be prepared to do the work. There is a good chance that God has a lot to teach you in those mucky trenches as well.

If you feel like there is something missing in

your life, like you're longing for something more, I'm going to save you some time. It's Jesus. That's whom you are craving. It is a desire built into our souls before we were formed in our mother's womb. We were made to crave Him.

If you're ready for recovery, if you're tired of living in your eating disorder, get ready for a battle. The enemy will not let recovery come easy. He knows your weaknesses and how to tempt you. Equip yourself with God's truths. Put on the full armor of God daily.

Finally, be strong in the Lord and in His mighty power. Put on the full armor of God, so that you can take your stand against the devil's schemes. For our struggle is not against flesh and blood, but against the rulers, against the authorities, against the powers of this dark world and against the spiritual forces of evil in the heavenly realms. Therefore put on the full armor of God, so that when the day of evil comes, you may be able to stand your ground, and after you have done everything, to stand.

Stand firm then, with the belt of truth buckled around your waist, with the breastplate of righteousness in place, and with your feet

with the readiness that comes from the el of peace. In addition to all this, take up the shield of faith, with which you can extinguish all the flaming arrows of the evil one. Take the helmet of salvation and the sword of the Spirit, which is the word of God.
Ephesians 6:10-17 (NIV)

Lastly, don't try to do this on your own. Seek professional help. Do your best to form a support system. Listen to those professionals and follow their treatment plans. Alongside of all of that, walk with Jesus. He will never leave you nor forsake you. He will be with you every step of that uphill battle and on the days when you feel like giving up, He will carry you if you let Him.

I'm going to close this by sharing a portion of a letter I wrote as my time in treatment was coming to a close. It's been something that I keep close by as a reminder that any Goliath I face is never bigger than the God who redeemed me.

When I came to treatment for anorexia in Birmingham, Alabama, I was like a scared little girl cowering in the dark corner entangled in chains that I believed were a permanent part of my body. The treatment center helped me to see that they weren't permanent. They helped guide me as I discovered what the chains consisted of and challenged me when I tried to avoid the most painful and uncomfortable ones. They patiently pushed through my defiant and skeptical attitude and showed me that they really were there to support me in my recovery and that this is much more than a job for each of them. They supported me as I faced my greatest fear: vulnerability. They supported me as I sat with that fear and found the strength within myself to stand up from that corner.

It was after that, that I realized that alongside my own strength, I needed the strength that only Jesus could give me and that strength was what broke the chains. That is what allows me to now hold these broken chains high, not as boasting of what I've been through or what I've overcome, but as boasting of what I have been set free from because of Jesus with the prayer that they will radiate hope and unconditional love to others.

Like a soldier ready for battle, I feel equipped to continue to face the ups and downs with the support of God and those He places in my life. As in the battle in which a giant was conquered it's a slingshot and a stone, I've gone from identifying with the fear filled soldiers standing opposite of Goliath, to identifying with the unlikely candidate of small David who ignored the words of others telling him that he wasn't capable, and trusted that God would be faithful to His promise. Then the most unlikely candidate defeated what seemed like an insurmountable opponent with the most unlikeliest of weapons.

We are all David. We all have people around us telling us that we aren't capable. We have that inner critic that brings doubt to the table. We all have times in which even those closest to us will doubt, just as David's brothers did. But we also have the opportunity to trust and accept that through Jesus we can stand strong amidst that controversy and be confident in the strength and courage that are grounded in that firm foundation. We all get to decide whom to listen to. We all choose whether our next step is forward or backward each time a new Goliath crosses our path.

The treatment team pushed me to step forward and helped me find my slingshot. God provides me with an unending supply of stones.

The giants may come, but because of Jesus I am equipped to take a step forward in the face of them.

RESOURCES

NEDA toll free, confidential helpline: 1-800-931-2237

For crisis situations, text "NEDA" to 741741 and you will be connected to a trained volunteer at Crisis Text Line.

Visit www.nationaleatingdisorders.org to chat with a NEDA Helpline volunteer, to find more information about eating disorders, to find out how you can help, or to find treatment centers near you.

Made in the USA
Lexington, KY
24 June 2016